Saving Michael:
A BULIMIA STORY

The true story of our Bulimic son,
and the powerful intervention of the Living God

Jon Hunter, with Sherry Hunter

ISBN 978-1-63575-698-2 (Paperback)
ISBN 978-1-63575-699-9 (Digital)

Christian Faith Publishing, Inc.
296 Chestnut Street
Meadville, PA 16335
www.christianfaithpublishing.com

Printed in the United States of America

When the darkness comes, and
life is beyond what you can bear,
don't be afraid; God is there.

norexia, bulimia, binge eating disorder—
A silent curse that exists in the lives of
many people today. Young people who are
desperate for acceptance. Women *and* men who
want to fit into the world's ideology of looking
thin and beautiful. The pressure on young teens
all the way up to middle-aged adults and beyond
is oppressive. People are dying, trying to become
acceptable to their peers.

Some who are affected by this modern-day
plight are just looking to gain control of their
everyday lives.

Most people fail to understand how dangerous
an eating disorder is. Between one and two percent
of young women in this country suffer from bulimia,
and one out of four people who are hospitalized from
problems associated with the disease will ultimately
die from it.

A painful question coming from parents today
might be: why us? Why our child? If this is a
question you are asking, the Lord of all creation has
an answer: God loves and cares about your loved
one even more than you do. He also loves you, and
He understands what you are going through. God
wants you to trust Him, *especially* when the pain of

your situation overwhelms you and you feel hopeless. Nothing is too hard for the Lord to handle. His wisdom and power far exceed our understanding. If you or a loved one is suffering with an eating disorder or *any* problem that dominates your life, then perhaps God has sent this story to you.

CHAPTER 1

Chastening—a period of painful instruction sent from God. Mine began the moment that the Lord decided to teach me to trust and rely on Him in a real and powerful way. Hebrews 12:5–6 says, "My son, despise not thou the chastening of the Lord, nor faint when thou art rebuked of him: For whom the Lord loveth he chasteneth, and scourgeth every son whom he receiveth." God knows where our heart is, and sometimes He grabs our attention using what is surely the most valuable possession in our lives. Sometimes He uses our children.

It began when Michael, our youngest son, was just a boy. God allowed a number of significant changes to occur in my life to lift me up. Afterward, He permitted me to slip into a deep pit of despair. This pit was prepared for me because of the apathetic attitude that I had developed toward the things of God. My reaction to the events that the Lord brought into my life had a profound effect on my family's lives, especially on the life of my youngest son, Michael.

In 1982, I was a twenty-seven-year-old father-to-be who had not yet really matured enough to be a parent. Our firstborn son, Gabriel, was on the way, and Michael, who would be our youngest, was still just a distant thought.

Sherry, my wife, had an excellent job as a purchasing expediter for a large beverage distribution company. She was the levelheaded one in our marriage, the one who kept me in line. I was more of the risk-taker, which really means that I was careless when it came to finances and life decisions in general.

I was employed by an engineering firm in Columbus, Ohio, whose business had declined because of the early 1980s recession. I had been working as a draftsman for eight years and thought it might be time to seek out a new, more lucrative career.

Sherry's administrator was responsible for the hiring and firing of the building service contractors for her company. She told Sherry one day how lucrative the building service industry was. When Sherry shared this information with me, I realized what a great opportunity such a business might offer.

I decided to contact the person in charge of my company's building services to see if they might consider hiring me as an independent contractor to provide the janitorial services for our building. Because business was sluggish, I thought that I could offer a more affordable service package to my employer to lure them into using me. I was hoping to slowly transition into this new business venture of mine without leaving my current employment.

It was just a few days later on a Friday afternoon that I received the unfortunate news that I was being permanently laid off from my job. This was an event that I didn't anticipate happening. The following Monday, I was awarded the contract to clean my employer's forty-thousand-square-foot building. Remarkably, God had placed me into the commercial cleaning business.

I could definitely see God's hand in this and was excited and thankful that the decision to leave my job was taken out of my hands. Unfortunately, Sherry wasn't as excited as I was. With a baby on the way, she felt that this new business venture was very risky.

I had strong confidence though, that God was in control of this new opportunity and that this business was what He wanted me to pursue. The Lord immediately began to open the doors of blessing for Sherry and me.

Within just a couple of weeks, we had the opportunity to start providing cleaning services for a church that the president of the engineering firm I had been employed with attended. Sherry's company also hired me to provide the janitorial service for their building. Soon we began offering home cleaning services in several North Columbus suburbs, which turned out to be an opportunity waiting to explode. After four years, our small company had grown to employ nearly thirty people.

In 1985, we were blessed with our second and youngest son, Michael, just three years after Gabriel, our eldest, was born.

Two years after Michael arrived, we were approached by a gentleman who expressed interest in buying our business. He had been a successful businessman who opted for early retirement and wanted to try his hand at running his own business.

After much thought, Jim offered to buy our young but growing company under the condition that I would stay with him as his general manager. He also wanted to hire Sherry to manage his residential cleaning division. I was thrilled. It seemed as though everything was going our way. Life had become exciting and easy for Sherry and me. Unfortunately, my attitude had become somewhat worldly. I wasn't living in outrageous sin, but my first priority in life wasn't my fellowship with God anymore.

It's easy to lose focus on a relationship with the Lord when everything is comfortable in life. The pleasantries of the world can seem very satisfying for a moment, but they tend to draw a person away from God. Eventually, the Lord will do whatever He needs to do to gain our attention and to bring us back to Him. It can be a very unpleasant, even painful, position for a Christian to be in.

Historically, our company's sales had doubled every ten months. This steady growth continued during the first year that Jim, the new owner of our business, took control.

For the first six months after the sale, Jim treated me like a prince. During that period, he bathed me in flatteries and encouragement.

Precisely six months later at the beginning of 1987, everything changed. Jim turned against me. Although Jim had been a successful leader in the business world, he failed at keeping his finances under control. I had become just another big expense in his overburdened budget. Soon Jim decided that he didn't need me any longer.

For the next six months, he tried everything he could to motivate me to resign. I was just one year into my new management position when he finally fired me. Sherry and I had just built a new home, which was a risky thing to do during this career transition of mine. It wasn't very long before we were in a financial crisis and my self-esteem plummeted. To make my dismissal even more humbling was that Sherry was still employed by Jim and seemed to be doing quite well. In one additional year, though, Jim let Sherry go also.

We were soon forced to sell our new home, taking our children away from their schools and friends. I had to accept a job making one fourth of my former salary. It felt as though God had turned against me. Life had seemed so easy, but now *nothing* was working out. In all of this, God was silent. I didn't know what to do. I was mad at life and frustrated with God. I became paranoid and very controlling. My depression flowed like a foul stream in front of my wife and kids. It seemed as though I was always angry. I was drowning in guilt, feeling like I had failed my family. All the while, our financial struggles seemed endless, and my paranoia continued to grow.

We had moved into a small rental townhouse after selling the home we had just built. When Sherry was fired by Jim, she immediately found a new career opportunity. I was fortunate to finally be hired again as a draftsman with another engineering firm.

Eventually, we were able to buy a small home in Delaware County, Ohio, in the growing town of Lewis Center. At the time, Delaware County was the fastest growing county in the United States. Lewis Center was a rural community with excellent schools. It wasn't long before our boys settled down and developed new friendships.

During that period, a number of high-end housing communities were under development in the desirable Olentangy School District, and young professionals flocked to the region. As our children knew, we were at the lower end of the financial scale in the area.

After our move, I had an idea to open a small carpet cleaning business. I discussed this thought with Sherry during lunch one day. Again she wasn't as enthusiastic as I was about me being self-employed, and again the following day, I was permanently laid off from my drafting position at the engineering firm that I was employed with. I was given six weeks' severance pay, which I felt was just enough time to start my new business. I soon found out that this new venture turned out to be a constant struggle. God didn't make things as easy for me as He did when we started our first business.

CHAPTER 2

I had wanted to give our children some of the niceties that the more affluent children had, probably to make myself feel better about me. All that I accomplished was to bury Sherry and myself deeper into debt. I didn't want my boys to feel deprived just because of my lack of education and ability to provide a nice life for them.

As my boys grew, I had the normal worries that parents have. I was especially concerned about either of them becoming involved with alcohol or drugs.

When he was fifteen, my oldest son, Gabriel, was caught with alcohol in his possession at a church summer camp. My distrust had become a self-fulfilling prophecy.

By the time Gabriel had turned eighteen, he was smoking pot *and* drinking. I didn't know what to do. Life had become a constant struggle. I saw my oldest son's life heading in the wrong direction. Everything seemed to be spiraling out of control.

I think that my lack of faith in God and my weakness as a father created a sense of insecurity in my youngest son, Michael. Because I had been *so* controlling, he had grown to depend on me to have solutions for all of these problems, but unfortunately, I didn't.

Troubles with his older brother, our financial issues, and problems that I had created between his mother and me all whittled away at his sense of security. It seemed that Michael saw my weakness and felt that *his* life was also out of control.

For years, Michael had been the epitome of the strong-willed child. He was *always* pushing buttons to get attention. He was very intelligent, popular with friends, and an active fifteen-year-old.

Like most older brothers, Gabriel didn't like being bothered by Michael very much. He had his "older brother" friends and activities and didn't want Michael to be involved in that part of his life. It seemed as though there were always clashes between the two.

When Gabriel was seventeen years old, he started lifting weights and became very serious about bodybuilding. Michael wanted to be involved with Gabe's workouts, but I discouraged it. I felt that

Michael was too young to work out and that Gabe deserved his privacy.

I also thought that Michael was again just wanting attention. I was constantly trying to stay one step ahead of him in his attempts to get attention. I know that I made him feel less wanted than his older brother.

Michael was annoyed with Gabe because of his drug and alcohol use and jealous because he was very popular with girls and had the freedoms that an older brother has. This created an even bigger division between them. He always felt like he was in competition with Gabe. I believe that because Gabriel was so trim, Michael felt inferior.

CHAPTER 3

When Michael was fifteen years old, he was stocky. He wasn't fat, but he wasn't skinny either. At five feet, six inches tall, he weighed around 185 pounds. Not only did Michael feel inferior to Gabe because of his body image, but he also suffered from cruel comments that he had received from others about his weight. One boy insinuated that Michael had feminine breasts.

That one particular remark affected Michael so severely that it scarred him for life. He never got over it. He never again believed that his body was normal. We all have heard the saying that "words will never hurt me," but that is so untrue. The "breast" comment was the beginning of the end of Michael's life. It was then that Michael decided to make some drastic changes to his body.

Toward the end of the year 2000, Michael started dieting. This took tremendous willpower because Michael loved to eat. He especially enjoyed going to buffet restaurants with Sherry and me. Michael had become very determined to lose weight. He modified his eating habits, and the pounds just seemed to roll off. It wasn't long before *he* started catching glances from girls and receiving flattering comments from his friends.

We also were amazed at his progress, and at first we gave him a lot of positive support, but there came a point during this period that Michael's dieting became an obsession. It was a dark obsession that eventually took complete control of his life. Michael became extremely thin.

Sherry and I were worried. Michael had reduced his calorie intake to between just two hundred and four hundred calories each day. We were told that a teenage boy would burn seventeen hundred calories in a day just lying in bed.

He also had secretly developed an addiction to ephedrine, a powerful stimulant which could be purchased at health supplement stores at that time. Michael had stolen a state photo ID that belonged to his brother, and he looked enough like Gabriel to use the ID to buy the stimulant.

Ephedrine suppressed his appetite and gave him the energy he needed to function. Michael took many times the recommended dosage, a dangerous thing to do *especially* when he was barely eating.

After about six months of Michael's dieting, we decided to seek medical advice because his weight loss had become so extreme. We were referred to a physician who had been anorexic when she was in college. She examined Michael and, after doing blood work, determined that immediate hospitalization was necessary. Michael's potassium and sodium levels had become dangerously low. His weight also had plummeted to one hundred and five pounds. Michael had lost eighty pounds in just six months.

Sherry took Michael to Children's Hospital in Columbus where they have an eating disorder unit for young people. Michael was examined by one of the physicians there, and that doctor agreed that Michael needed immediate medical attention.

Sherry called me from the hospital and told me that Michael had to be admitted to Children's Hospital or he might die. The doctor told her that a teenager suffering from a severe eating disorder is five hundred times more likely to have a heart attack or stroke than an obese adult.

The subject of eating disorders was relatively new to Sherry and me, so the severity of Michael's condition came as quite a shock.

I was working at the home of a dear Christian missionary couple when Sherry called me. God was very kind in allowing me to be with other believers when she called. I shared with Gene and Mildred what Sherry had told me and how serious Michael's condition had become. They prayed with me for God's merciful intervention and for Michael's healing.

When Michael found out that he was going to be admitted to Children's Hospital, he was furious. I've been told that sometimes an eating disorder is caused by a need for control. Michael was determined that he would be in control of his own life and to lose as much weight as he wanted to. No one was going to stop him in his quest to do so. He also tried to convince us that God didn't want him to be put in the hospital.

His drive to lose weight was so extreme that he had become like a stranger to Sherry and me, not the happy fifteen-year-old son we had known just six months earlier. Michael *was* admitted to Children's Hospital and was told that he needed to stay hospitalized until he gained at least eight pounds.

We went to visit Michael every day to support him and also to keep a close eye on his progress. When meal time arrived, all of the patients in his unit were watched carefully to make sure that the food that was eaten stayed in the body and was not "vomited" out.

We were amazed to see how strong the distorted body image was in the minds of these young people. It was almost all young women who were there, and though they were grievously thin, they still believed that they were overweight. You could see the desperation in their faces as they tried to deal with their illness.

Michael could see how deceived they were about their bodies, but yet he couldn't accept the fact that he was deceived about his own. Each day that we visited him, he would again try to convince us that he wasn't supposed to be in the hospital. It was very draining emotionally for Sherry and me.

It took ten days for Michael to gain the eight pounds he needed to be discharged. He was finally released from Children's Hospital, making promises of eating healthy meals again and reaching a nominal weight, which, according to doctors, should have been around one hundred forty pounds. The head physician in the eating disorder unit told us that he didn't think that Michael was anorexic, but that he was just very good at dieting.

We had great hopes that after Michael's hospitalization, he would straighten up and get on with his life. Unfortunately, things became progressively worse.

CHAPTER 4

At about this time, I decided to buy Michael a motorcycle. One of my many bad decisions as a father. I hoped that it might take his mind off of dieting. Michael had already owned a dirt bike for a couple of years and had ridden over two thousand miles in our little one-and-a-half-acre yard. He had not yet owned a street bike.

I was amazed to find out that in Ohio, a fifteen-year-old could obtain a temporary riding permit for a motorcycle and ride non-freeway roads without supervision. Michael loved to ride his bike, and he did it like a pro. I bought him a sport bike. This particular bike had two drawbacks—one being that it was easy to pull up the front of the bike and ride "wheelies," which Michael loved to do and was very good at, and the other was that this bike could travel at up to 160 miles per hour, something that Michael had actually tried on rural roads near our home. Sherry and I also rode motorcycles but in a much slower and safer manner.

It seemed as though my plan was working, and Michael's focus was on riding his bike instead of losing weight.

Everything appeared to be going better, but things aren't always as they seem. Michael started eating normal foods again. In fact, he *really* started eating. I suspect that he learned something new from his association with some of the other patients at Children's Hospital.

I am not quite sure when we first noticed the vomiting, which I will refer to as "purging" from this point on, but it wasn't more than a month after he was discharged from Children's Hospital.

I remember waking one night about midnight and noticing that our kitchen light appeared to be on. I quietly walked out to see what was happening, and found Michael standing at the kitchen sink. He was gorging himself with slices of plain bread and then "purging" the bread into the kitchen sink disposal. He didn't appear to be eating for the pleasure of eating. He was eating rather for the pleasure of purging! He had finished his first loaf and was working on the second loaf when I caught him.

I was heartsick. Because of my lack of understanding about the forces that were driving

Michael's eating disorder, I was now dealing with the fear that he might be mentally ill. I told Michael that the purging needed to stop and that I thought that he was acting like an animal.

Michael's reaction was very strange. It was almost as if he was in a trance. I came to understand years later that when a bulimic purges their food, antidepressants are released into the brain, creating a type of euphoric state of mind. This is one reason why bulimia is so addictive. Michael had traveled even further in his new journey toward death.

It became very hard to maintain our own sanity, watching this illness take control of his life. The signs of Michael's bulimia were everywhere. His bathroom became absolutely disgusting. The purge would get on the floor, on the wall, all over his toilet, even on his shoes. One afternoon while putting away clean clothing in his bedroom, I found a large, heavy duty trash bag hanging in his closet. It contained several gallons of "purge" that he was saving, almost like a trophy of calories that he didn't completely digest. Michael became more and more obsessed with binge eating. He started skipping school. Instead, he would go to Walmart carrying empty plastic grocery bags in his pocket. He would fill the bags with his favorite binge foods, commonly large bags of sugar cereal and a couple gallons of milk, and then simply walk out of the store without being noticed.

He would take the food home to binge and purge over and over again and then flush out his body with gallons of water to make sure that no food remained in his system.

Michael was so thorough at cleansing his body of food that he would go for days, or even weeks, without having a normal bowel movement. He was also taking laxatives every day to assist in his weight control.

On two different occasions, Michael was caught stealing food at local grocery stores. Michael was permanently banned from the Walmart we shopped at. He was charged with shoplifting on the second occasion and on that occasion was forced to appear before a judge, but he dropped the shoplifting charges when he found out about Michael's illness.

I want to stress that at this period in Michael's illness, I believe that it was by God's grace that he was still alive. A middle-aged business associate of mine who knew Michael and understood how dangerous his bulimia was, actually became bulimic herself after seeing Michael's weight loss. She decided to try purging to lose weight. It was less than a year later that she died from its horrible effects. The sister of a close friend of Michael's also chose purging as a way of attempting to lose weight. I believe that through counseling, she was able to free herself from the addiction, but giving up the habit can be very difficult. It is frightening that a person can be driven to such extremes to become thin, knowing the potential dangers that come with it.

The first time that Michael was admitted to Children's Hospital, he weighed just 105 pounds. He was now continuing to lose weight.

CHAPTER 5

Between the years 2001 and 2004, Michael was hospitalized six different times because his potassium and sodium levels had become critically low. Every time that we had to put him in the hospital was a battle. He would always be angry and very defiant.

On one particular occasion, he was once again sent to Children's Hospital. I had been warning him that if his potassium level was found to be too low, he would have to be admitted to the hospital.

We had taken him to his doctor for blood work, and it was determined that he needed treatment. Michael was enraged when he found out he was being admitted. He decided to run away from Children's, which is located in a dangerous area of Columbus. The police were called, and by God's grace, Michael was found unharmed, walking around one of the streets near the hospital. The police forced him to return to his hospital room, and a guard was placed outside of his door to make sure that he didn't run off again. He was discharged two days later. When Sherry picked him up and was driving him back to the house, he threatened several times to jump out of the car, opening his door while riding on the freeway.

When they did arrive home, he was so crazed and belligerent that I was forced to call the Delaware County sheriff's office. He was now sixteen years old, and the deputies told me that I could spank him if I felt the need to, but that was about all that I could do legally. They talked to him for about an hour but to no avail.

His mental condition combined with his addiction to ephedrine (which we still did not know about) made living with him almost unbearable. We even talked to an attorney because we were considering making him a ward of the courts.

Michael was so obsessed with his addiction that after a while, he completely stopped going to school. The school district sent tutors to our home to try and help him complete his eleventh grade year, but he was not able or willing to do so.

The school nurse finally contacted Children's Services because of Michael's condition. They in turn contacted us to meet with Michael, Sherry, and me. They were wanting to find out what was going on with Michael's weight loss and health.

The social worker was very understanding. After meeting with Michael, he realized that what was happening was out of our control. He worked with Sherry to obtain Medicaid assistance for Michael's medical bills. He also helped us connect with the Delaware County Department of Health to see if there was any counseling or psychiatric assistance that could be provided. A county psychiatrist did become involved in Michael's case.

We started taking Michael to meet with him once a week. The doctor prescribed several medications to help him sleep and to assist with his depression issues. But after just a few counseling sessions, it was determined that Michael needed to be placed in inpatient care. Unfortunately, the costs associated with inpatient treatment were not covered by our health insurance policy *or* by Medicaid, and the expense of an inpatient clinic was prohibitive. It was very discouraging that Michael's health coverage would pay for virtually unlimited hospital treatment when his body chemistry got out of whack, but it wouldn't pay for inpatient care, which, in the long run, would have been considerably less expensive.

From seemingly out of nowhere, the Delaware County Department of Health secured fifty thousand dollars, which could be used for Michael's inpatient treatment. Sherry and I were thrilled, but of course, Michael wasn't.

It wasn't until I came home in the middle of the day a few days later, and caught him in the middle of a binge episode, that I finally convinced him that he needed to go to an inpatient clinic for treatment.

Sherry and I began our search to find a clinic that would be able to help our son. Our search narrowed quickly when we found out that only three inpatient clinics in the entire country would accept males as patients. Sherry contacted the three and chose the one which was the most affordable, Rogers Memorial Hospital in Oconomowoc, Wisconsin.

They soon had an opening for Michael, so we made our plans to go. The next couple of weeks were very tense while we waited to leave.

A couple of days prior to going, Michael and I got into an altercation. He had become so rude and cocky with us. When I confronted him about it, he clenched his fist as if he were going to punch me. I grabbed him by the shoulders and forced him onto his bed and held him down. I told him that he needed to get himself under control. He showered me with some of the most profane names and words that a son could call his father.

I released him and walked out of the room. When he came out of his bedroom, he called me a few more names and walked out of our home.

He returned about thirty minutes later and apologized. It was then that he told us about his use of the stimulant ephedrine. He believed that it had a lot to do with his horrible and profane attitude.

I'm sure that his physical condition added to his anger. Michael must have felt horrible physically as well as emotionally. He was also very anxious about going to the inpatient clinic. I too was anxious that Michael might end up refusing to go on the trip with us, and I didn't have a clue as to how we could force him to go if he chose not to. Sherry and I had to leave that in God's hands.

In making plans for our trip, we decided to leave Columbus on a Saturday morning, fly into Chicago's Midway Airport, and stay at an airport hotel. On Monday, we would drive a rental car from Chicago to Rogers Memorial. I was relieved and thankful that Michael cooperated with us and went on the trip. I had purchased a new laptop computer for him to take along, which firmed up his decision to go. I was using it as a bribe to help motivate him to keep his commitment to us.

We flew out of Columbus, arriving in Chicago early Saturday morning, and went to our hotel. I don't recall why we decided to go to Chicago two days before his admission to the clinic, but it was a bad idea because we had to deal with Michael's stress for those two days. Even though he had initially agreed to receive treatment, we understood that neither Rogers Memorial nor either of the other two clinics would allow anyone over fourteen years of age to be admitted against their will.

Sherry and I wanted to do something fun with Michael while we were in Chicago. We were hoping to take the edge off of his fears a little about going into the clinic. We decided to travel on the elevated train to visit what at that time was the Sears Tower. We wanted to go to the observation floor to view the expanse of downtown Chicago and then afterward check out what kind of shopping we could find in the area.

We were able to catch a train at a terminal right beside the hotel. It was our first time going to the downtown area. I was a little nervous about how safe it would be to take the train. I had always heard that subways and elevated train systems can be dangerous because of street tuffs and criminals, but I figured that on a sunny Saturday afternoon, we would be all right.

As we headed toward downtown, Michael began to make conversation with anyone on the train that he could, telling people that he had *been* bulimic but that God had healed him. This little bit of information was certainly news to Sherry and me.

After about thirty minutes, we arrived at the tower and traveled to the observation floor. Michael seemed very reserved. You could tell that he was wanting to escape this whole clinic situation. His focus was unquestionably on how he could get out of being admitted and not much else.

The view of Chicago was amazing. It was quite a change from downtown Columbus. When you are high above the city looking out at the world, it's easy to forget about all of life's problems for just a little while. Eventually, though, all of those problems come back into focus, and you have to face reality, and the reality of our situation was that if this clinic didn't help Michael, we were beaten.

Michael was much too nervous about going to the clinic to enjoy anything. We traveled back down to the street level, hoping to find a good place to have dinner. We stopped at a restaurant and had sandwiches (which after eating, Michael didn't purge) and then headed back to the hotel. I think that by not purging his meal he was also trying to convince Sherry and me that his bulimia was gone.

Again while on the train, Michael spoke with anyone who would listen to him, telling them that God had healed him of his disorder.

We finally settled down back at the hotel for Saturday evening, Michael in his room and Sherry and I in ours.

CHAPTER 6

I t was around twelve thirty in the morning when my cell phone rang. It was Michael calling me. He said, "Dad, I wanted to let you know that I'm on the train."

"What?" I asked.

"I said I'm on the train," he responded.

"Why?" I questioned, not knowing how that could be. I thought that Michael didn't have any money, and I couldn't imagine where he would be heading on the train in the middle of the night. I could hear a commotion in the background.

"Shut up!" Michael barked.

"Were you talking to me?" I asked.

"No, Dad...*Shut up!*" At that point, Michael told me that there were four guys on the train that were trying to mug him. *They* were the ones that he was yelling at.

By this time, Michael's weight had dropped to around ninety-five pounds. He was weak at best. He was carrying with him his new laptop computer, his watch, a PayPal card, fifty cents cash, and a pocketful of laxatives. Because of his weakened condition, he wasn't thinking clearly. He would instead speak out of anger, not using good judgment when talking to the young men.

I was terrified. I could hear the wild temperament of the thugs harassing my son. I was convinced that I would hear Michael be beaten up, or even killed, while we were on the phone.

By now, Sherry was awake. I told her what was going on, so she quickly called the front desk of the hotel seeking help in contacting the police. The front desk personnel agreed that Michael was in a very dangerous situation. No one wants to be on the elevated train in Chicago in the middle of a Saturday night.

At some point in the conversation, Michael said to me, "Dad, let me call you back." That's when something amazing happened. I believe that God spoke to me, not audibly, but I believe that He spoke to my heart, saying "You're helpless. You're going to have to depend on Me."

Suddenly, the fear left me, and I had peace. I knew then that God had complete control of the situation that Michael was in. I also knew that if Michael was hurt or killed, it was what God had planned for him. It was just a few minutes later that Michael called me back. The train had come to a stop. Michael hopped off, and the thugs didn't follow him. He was all right.

Someone helped Michael get on a train heading back toward the hotel, and he finally met me in the lobby. He told me that he was running away. He was heading downtown hoping to catch a bus home using his PayPal account to pay for a ticket. The guys on the train appeared to have full intentions of robbing him. They went through his pockets and told him that they were going to take his new computer, his watch, his shoes, his fifty cents, and his pills. The only thing they did steal from him were his laxative pills. I hope they swallowed *all* of them.

He did tell me that as scared as he was dealing with those young men on the train, he was a thousand times more frightened to go to the clinic the following Monday. I believe that God put those individuals on the train to force Michael to return to us at the hotel. This is just one of many ways that the Lord clearly intervened to protect Michael and to save his life. Now we just needed to get him to the clinic on Monday.

CHAPTER 7

Monday morning finally arrived. It had been a long, very tense weekend in Chicago. We had changed hotels after the first night to take away Michael's access to the train. We packed our bags and made the trip to Rogers Memorial.

When we arrived at the clinic and stepped out of the car, Michael started looking around like a cornered animal might do. The hospital was located in a rural setting, and I think that he was checking to see if he did decide to run away, where he could go to escape.

When we finally went inside, one of the physicians greeted us and took Michael into his office to talk with him privately. Sherry and I sat in the lobby, praying that Michael would agree to be admitted. After about an hour, the doctor called us into his office.

Michael now seemed to be displaying an entirely different personality. He was claiming that there had been a past issue in the clinic involving sexual improprieties with a former patient. Michael was grasping at any possible excuse he could to avoid being admitted. Supposedly because of this, he refused to stay and be treated.

We begged him to change his mind, asking him to try staying for just a week, but he wouldn't do it. We were beaten and we were trapped. Trapped because Michael's bulimia not only controlled his life but it controlled our lives as well. It dominated our very existence. We saw no hope for Michael unless God intervened in a miraculous way. We all headed back to Columbus that afternoon, not knowing what the future held, but God knew.

CHAPTER 8

Mother's Day 2004 arrived. Michael loved his mother, so Michael loved Mother's Day. He had always enjoyed doing nice things for Sherry.

It had now been about eight months since our trip to Wisconsin. Michael had turned eighteen years old, and his health had continued to deteriorate. I am sure that by now he was very close to dying.

Because he was so thin, he was always chilly, even in the warm spring sunshine. It could be sunny and sixty-five degrees outside, and he would still want to light the fireplace in our living room. Michael would commonly dress in layers, not just because he was cold but also because the clothing would help to hide his weight. This is very common for those who are seriously afflicted with anorexia or bulimia.

Michael had become so thin that when people saw him, I'm sure that they thought he had a terminal illness. His face looked like skin stretched tightly over a skull. The veins in his forehead bulged out in a freakish sort of way.

Sherry and I really didn't know for sure how thin Michael had become or to what level his health had deteriorated, but we did believe that his time was short. Because Michael had turned eighteen years old, we couldn't make him go to the hospital anymore. Frankly, sending him to the hospital only prolonged the inevitable. Michael refused to be helped, and his mind was made up.

It's tragic that a person who abuses illegal drugs can be forced into rehabilitation, but there isn't a law to keep a person from starving themselves to death. Sherry and I were completely helpless.

We began Mother's Day morning by taking Sherry to Bob Evans Restaurant for breakfast. As was commonly the case, Michael's demeanor was less than pleasant. Mental and emotional deterioration is common for people with severe eating disorders because the brain tends to shrink due to malnutrition. I casually made a suggestion as to what Michael might order for breakfast, and he reminded me that he didn't appreciate being told what to eat. He was very sensitive and had been hard to live with for a long time. We tried to enjoy our meal, but as always, things were tense.

After we were finished with breakfast, I went home to prepare my equipment for the upcoming week, while Sherry and Michael drove to downtown Columbus to watch the imploding of a wing of Grant Hospital. Sherry parked as close to the hospital as possible to watch the demolition. When it was over, she had to drive to where she and Michael had been watching, to pick Michael up. He was too weak to walk back to the car.

They arrived back home and sat out on our patio enjoying the beautiful sunny spring day. Later that afternoon, I took Michael out to look at new cars just for something to do. He always enjoyed looking at and test driving new cars, dreaming that one day he would own something exotic to drive. His mental condition was not good, and it worried me when he got behind the wheel. When he did drive, he always drove too fast.

When he and I arrived home, he took his spot in the living room in his favorite recliner. He had become too feeble to walk up our stairs to get to his bedroom, so he slept downstairs. He commonly didn't sleep very well, so he would nap a lot and sit and watch television.

Michael had shown signs of being obsessive-compulsive for a long time. He had developed a regular routine for almost everything. Each evening at a set time, he would take a nap. He wanted to be woken at the same time afterward, fifty-five minutes later, when he would then eat a low-calorie frozen dinner. Afterward, he would, of course, purge the few calories that he had eaten, and then he would head back to his recliner.

Every day was basically the same routine. Michael had no plans or goals. I believe that he was just waiting to die. Sherry and I, with a lack of anything else that we could do for him, were trying to make his life as pleasant and comfortable as possible.

When supper time arrived, we all rode our motorcycles to an area restaurant for dinner. Riding a motorcycle was something that Michael should now not have been doing because he was much too feeble to ride safely.

When we were done eating, Sherry and I got on our bikes and headed home, while Michael waited to get into the restroom to purge his dinner. When Sherry and I were about halfway home, Michael caught up with us and passed us, traveling at more than one hundred miles an hour. I thought to myself right then that he was going to die on his bike if the bulimia didn't kill him first.

CHAPTER 9

When Mother's Day evening arrived, Michael wanted to go and buy doughnuts for desert to finish Sherry's special evening.

Michael and I arrived back at the house with the doughnuts at about eight thirty. Sherry was working on something in the kitchen when we got back home.

When we stepped into the house, Michael called in to Sherry from the living room. "Mom, are you ready for your doughnut?" Sherry didn't hear him, so I yelled to her more forcefully. "Sherry...do you want your doughnut?!"

I was irritated that Sherry didn't hear Michael when he called in to her. I was angry with Michael and tired of his bulimia.

I was tired of its control in our lives, and honestly, I was tired of waiting for Michael to die. I know that sounds horrible and heartless, but his problems absolutely consumed me.

I was confident that Michael was a believer in Christ. I know that a Christian can have a mental or emotional illness just as easily as they can have cancer or any other disease and still be a Christian.

I was used up. When I yelled in to Sherry, Michael responded, "Dad! Do you have to talk to Mom like that?"

I was done! I told him, "I don't need that," meaning that I didn't need him to tell *me* how to act when his actions in life were so bizarre. I went out to our garage, got on my motorcycle, and rode off toward the center of New Albany.

It was dusk as I rode across a nearby highway bridge, which was just a couple of miles from our home. As I rode, I started colliding with insects, lots of insects. I thought that maybe God was using this to tell me to turn around, so I made a U-turn and headed back home.

As I was riding, I saw Michael on his bike heading the other way looking for me. I was so tired and angry. We had lived with Michael's illness for three horrible years. I felt like I couldn't live with it any longer.

I looked up to Heaven from my bike, and I yelled to God. Actually out of anger, I yelled *at* God, saying, "Kill him! Why don't you just kill him?"

Michael had turned around and caught up to me at a stop sign. "Dad, can we talk?" he asked.

"No," I responded. "I don't feel like talking right now." *Tough love*, I thought to myself.

"Dad, please, can we talk?" He begged again.

"No, I *don't* want to talk right now!" I replied.

Michael, whether out of frustration or anger, turned left and opened up his bike. The street that he turned onto was a four-lane road that narrowed down to two lanes with a grassy median in the middle. Michael sped past a car on his left, heading toward the area where the road narrowed. After that, I wasn't really sure what happened because the car that he passed blocked my view. I could only see his motorcycle, sliding down the road on its side. I guessed that he was traveling at around seventy miles an hour when he fell.

I rode up to where I saw his bike stop, and there was Michael, lying in the middle of the road. *No helmet!* He wanted to catch up with me so badly that he didn't take time to put his helmet on! He lay there in the road, barely alive. Nothing but a skeleton covered in flesh.

I remembered that the last thing I said to Michael was that I wouldn't talk with him. Maybe the last words that I would *ever* say to my son. I also remembered yelling at God, "Kill him! Why don't you just kill him?"

I got off of my bike, knelt beside Michael, and cried out to God. I begged. "Lord Jesus, *please* save my son."

Almost immediately, there were ten or twelve people around us at the scene. One woman, who was a nurse, tried to make Michael as comfortable as possible. People were watching and praying for him.

An emergency squad had already been called. Soon a Columbus police officer came and closed the road but didn't come over to the accident scene. When the medics finally arrived and stepped out of the squad, it seemed as though they just stared at Michael's body. I think they knew that his chances for survival were almost nonexistent. What they didn't understand was that the living God had Michael's life in *His* hands. Beyond that, nothing else mattered.

The medics considered calling for a life flight helicopter to transport Michael but decided to take him to the hospital by squad.

I called Sherry and told her what had happened. She rushed to the scene and arrived just as they were loading Michael into the ambulance. The medics decided to take him to Riverside Methodist Hospital in Columbus.

We hurried back to our house to close things up and rushed to the hospital. I called my brother to ask him to pray for Michael that he might survive. Gene was a young adult Sunday school teacher in his church. He and his students, along with many others at his church, had been praying for Michael for a long time.

Sherry and I arrived at Riverside Hospital right behind the squad. We were led to a waiting area while Michael was taken into the emergency room. We weren't allowed to see him for quite a while. My brother and his wife, Janet, arrived at Riverside Hospital shortly after we did. We all knelt and prayed that the Lord might save Michael's life.

I felt that Michael's accident was my fault. If I had just talked with him when he asked me to, none of this would have happened. If I hadn't yelled at God to kill my son, *perhaps* none of this would have happened.

As I prayed, I asked God to spare Michael. I never really wanted him to die. I loved my son. I was just drained. I had reached the bottom of a deep emotional pit and felt trapped. Now I was drowning in guilt, feeling that I might be responsible for my son's death.

We were all directed to a different waiting area where a hospital pastor met with us. He was a multidenominational pastor who was sent to talk with us, probably because they were confident that Michael would die.

This poor man seemed very empty spiritually. I'm not sure that he knew Jesus personally, and I don't think he really understood the peace that we were experiencing. I'm sure that he had seen people lose loved ones many times, some who had no knowledge or hope of salvation or eternal life. I was confident that Michael was saved and that he and I would see each other again in Heaven if he did die. I'm so thankful to the Lord for the gift of eternal life and for salvation through Jesus by his grace alone.

Soon Michael's brother, Gabriel, arrived along with his wife and our two-week-old grandson, Levi. We sat and talked and waited.

Two officers from the New Albany Police department arrived at the hospital to take an accident report. The sergeant who came was very kind. He was wearing a cross and spoke as though he were a believer.

He brought a ball cap and a pair of sandals, which were found at the accident scene. Michael had been wearing the cap and the sandals when he fell. Both the bill of his cap and the toes of his sandals were embedded with mud. I believe that God in His tender mercy carefully controlled Michael's fall. Apparently, when he crashed, he fell into the grassy median and then rolled into the street. The median contained a line of small trees running along its center just feet away from the curb. If Michael would have hit one of those trees, he would have been killed instantly.

I knew that Michael was very close to dying from his bulimia. I had not considered that this accident might be God's way of saving his life.

CHAPTER 10

We weren't allowed to see Michael until early the next morning. At around seven thirty, someone took Sherry and me into the trauma unit where he was being cared for. He was still unconscious and in very critical condition.

We were told by the trauma room staff that when Michael was taken into the emergency room, the hospital personnel there had never seen anyone as thin as Michael in the hospital before. His weight had dropped close to seventy pounds.

Staff members came from other areas of the hospital to see him and to see what bulimia could do to a person. Mothers who had young daughters were the ones most concerned.

We were so impressed with the care that Michael received at Riverside Hospital. The normal ratio of nurses to patients in the trauma unit is one nurse for every two patients. They provided two nurses to care just for Michael.

After a multitude of tests were performed, they found that Michael was experiencing cranial bleeding. He needed surgery to relieve the increasing pressure, or he would die. This surgery was performed soon after the diagnosis was made. It now appeared that Michael might live, but he would suffer from the effects of a traumatic brain injury.

Michael was kept in intensive care for three and a half weeks. When he did regain consciousness and we were able to talk with him, though weak and extremely tired, he seemed to act almost normal, but we had no idea what we were really dealing with and what kind of effects a traumatic brain injury could have on a person.

After all that we had been through, we now had this new challenge to face. The important thing was that Michael was still alive.

CHAPTER 11

After five weeks, the decision was made to transfer Michael to Grant Hospital for rehabilitation. Grant Hospital was the hospital that he and Sherry had visited the day of his motorcycle accident. Michael seemed to be doing well during the first two days after arriving at Grant. He was able to rest comfortably and seemed to be calm. He needed to be in a quiet environment and required lots of rest. Sufferers of traumatic brain injuries need to be kept in a peaceful setting and should not be exposed to an excessive amount of activity while healing.

On Michael's third day at Grant Hospital, his personality changed. He became quiet and dysfunctional. He was not able to interact with anyone. He would just stare at the ceiling or sleep.

After two more days, Michael became more aware and very agitated. His demeanor became quite unpleasant. He also began to hallucinate. The hospital provided "sitters" to stay with him in his room twenty-four hours a day. Because of his condition, he began to say all sorts of inappropriate things to the sitters and to anyone else he saw. It was as though the part of his brain that limited or "curbed" what he might say was suddenly turned off.

Sherry and I were very disappointed with a few of the members of the rehabilitation staff at Grant Hospital. Most of the sitters and nursing techs were understanding and patient with Michael, but a few were much too sensitive to be working in that environment. It seemed as though the floor physician was more concerned about Michael offending one of the sitters by what he said than she was about helping him to heal.

The time came when this one particular doctor actually went into Michael's room and told him that he would have to leave the hospital if he didn't "straighten up and act right"! I don't believe that she took into consideration that Michael was in rehabilitation due to having a near fatal brain injury and that his language was completely out of his control.

We found out later that the symptoms that Michael was exhibiting were very typical for his type of brain injury. It seemed as though some of the rehabilitation staff at Grant Hospital didn't understand that.

I was quite concerned because if they did discharge Michael, we wouldn't know what to do with him. Sherry and I couldn't take him home to take care of him because he was mentally and physically dysfunctional.

What I didn't realize was that they *couldn't* discharge him legally without having somewhere else to send him to, so the doctor's threat to kick him out of the hospital was meaningless and cruel. Sherry was called into a physician's meeting soon after that to discuss Michael's condition. They told Sherry that "Michael might not get any better" and that his current condition was what we might be faced with permanently. We were devastated. Again God in His divine wisdom had a plan to help us.

CHAPTER 12

Soon a spot opened up for Michael at Dodd Hall, a rehabilitation unit at the Ohio State University Hospital. I had dropped off my work van for servicing and traveled by taxicab to Grant Hospital to visit Michael. A doctor at Grant told me about the opportunity that had opened up to move him to Dodd Hall. The doctors at Grant said that Dodd Hall was one of only four rehabilitation facilities of its caliber in the country. If Michael could be helped anywhere, Dodd was the place that he should be.

Michael and I left for Dodd Hall within a couple of hours. Instead of sending Michael to OSU by medical transport, they sent him and me by taxicab—something that I'll never understand considering his condition at that time.

Michael acted almost normal during the trip to Dodd Hall. This was a real answer to prayer because I was concerned that he might say something offensive to the driver.

When we arrived, I momentarily left Michael in the taxi and went in to the admissions desk to get a wheelchair. After speaking to the admissions personnel, I turned and saw Michael standing in the doorway, carrying his few possessions. Apparently, he was thinking clearly enough to come into the building on his own.

Michael was calm as we went up to the third floor nursing area. It wasn't until they put him in his room that he became agitated. He lay in his bed writhing. His brain wouldn't allow him to lie still and be calm. He was so unsettled that they had to strap him to the bedrails and sedate him.

Michael's new physician came into his room and spoke with me. He gave me new hope about Michael's recovery.

He understood that at this stage in Michael's healing, his condition was common for this type of brain injury. He told me that he had seen worse cases than Michael's and felt that with time he would improve.

Michael received amazing treatment at Dodd Hall. The staff was so professional and kind. I began to think that his medical team were angels sent from God.

During all of this, Michael was not showing any signs of still being bulimic. Because of his brain injury, the doctors at Dodd believed that he would be too mentally impaired to be controlled by his addiction anymore.

Michael began to gain a little weight, and though he was still thin, he started to look more normal and healthy again.

CHAPTER 13

After several weeks at Dodd Hall, Sherry and I took Michael to a local department store, which was close to the hospital, to get him out for a short while. When we walked into the store, he immediately went and hopped onto an electric wheelchair. We let him ride (closely monitored by us) around the store. What a thrill it was! It was almost like watching demolition derby.

There was Michael wearing his pajamas, buzzing around the store. He would rip around corners, clip displays, and race up the aisles at about two miles an hour. It was reminiscent of him riding his motorcycle, only much slower.

After five weeks at Dodd Hall, the day finally came for Michael to be discharged. It was July 20, 2004 when they let him go, two and a half months after he fell off of his bike. The rehabilitation staff threw a pizza party for him the day that he left. These wonderful people were such a blessing from God.

By the time that Michael was released, he had calmed down. He wasn't hallucinating anymore, and although he was not yet back to normal, he seemed to be happy and free. Possibly for the first time since he started dieting.

I was worried about whether or not Michael would cooperate with Sherry and me when we took him home. We still didn't know what kind of effects his brain injury would have on him once he left Dodd.

I had a solemn talk with Michael before we left the hospital. I made it very clear to him that he was welcome to come home and live with us but that he couldn't bring the bulimia with him. I really believe that he was relieved to hear that because it helped to curb any temptation he might face. It was tough love wrapped in a gentle package.

When he returned home, Michael seemed to function almost normally. He was loving and happy again. It was like getting our old son back.

Michael wasn't supposed to be left alone, so I started taking him to work with me. Sherry and I still owned our small carpet cleaning business, so I had the liberty to take him along. Sometimes he would help me a little with the work. Other times he would just stand and play games on my cell phone. I told all of my customers that Michael was my miracle son, how he had been severely bulimic and nearly died, but how God had intervened in his life and saved him.

Michael appeared to be healed. He was showing no signs of being bulimic, and after time, he seemed to have very few effects from the motorcycle accident. I think that the staff at Dodd Hall would have been amazed to see how well he had recovered. He continued to work with me every day and did quite well.

CHAPTER 14

Thanksgiving 2005 arrived. Over a year and a half had now passed since Michael's motorcycle accident. My brother Gene, my sister Margo, Gabriel, and their families met with Sherry, Michael and me at a restaurant to celebrate the holiday. After dinner, we sat and talked like families do.

After we finished eating, Michael had to get up for a restroom break. When he returned to the table, he leaned over to me and told me that he had been sick. I asked him if it was deliberate, and he said that he didn't know. I told him it was probably something bad that he had eaten and not to worry about it. I think I was trying to convince myself of that more than he.

It was just a day or so later that we heard Michael collapse. He was upstairs getting ready for bed. As he came out of his bathroom, he momentarily blacked out. I went up to help him, and I knew right away what was happening. I asked him what was going on. "Tell me the truth," I said.

"Well...I've been vomiting a little," he responded.

I couldn't believe it! I *thought* that God had healed my son. I *trusted* that God had healed my son. I *believed* in Him for Michael's healing, and now? For what? I felt beat up, punched, and dropped! I didn't know what to do or think. I don't believe that I had ever felt so let down. I told Michael that the purging was going to stop now! Well, again that wasn't the case.

I never should have blamed God for the sins of my son. I had to face and confess my own sin of having a critical and faithless attitude toward the Lord. I should not have assumed that God had permanently taken away Michael's bulimia because that's exactly what it was, an assumption. It would be no different than if Michael had been suffering from cancer which had gone into remission and returned when it was least expected.

It's very easy to blame God for the sins of others or for the horrible events that occur in life. God doesn't promise us a life without problems. In fact, as Christians, we have to expect challenging, possibly even horrible, painful times and events to enter our lives. God uses those times and events to teach us to be faithful to Him. How would we ever learn to seek and trust God if we didn't have a reason to?

It's those who don't see a need for a relationship with God that never learn to trust and depend on Him. It's God's love for us that motivates Him to chasten us. Through that chastening, He draws us close to Himself.

In all of my blaming God, He still remained so faithful and forgiving.

CHAPTER 15

Michael tried to hide his bulimia, but it was definitely back, not as ferociously as before but still back. I failed to boot him out of our home like I had threatened to because I knew that he couldn't survive on his own.

Michael worked with me daily and functioned pretty normally. He was very impulsive, a common problem caused by the traumatic brain injury. He started driving again and had a horrible road rage problem. He also started drinking. Alcohol became Michael's new friend. He spent quite a bit of time in bars close to where we lived.

It came to the point that I couldn't allow Michael to work with me anymore because his attitude had become too unpleasant. He tried working for several other employers—one being a large cable provider and another as a collector for a major financial institution.

At both jobs, Michael excelled, and even received recognition for his exceptional work. After a while, though, he would stop showing up for work so that he could spend the day drinking. Sometimes he would go to work still drunk from the night before. His drinking was just too much of a problem for him to function.

Alcohol and drug use, along with extreme impulsiveness, are common problems for many brain injury sufferers. I never thought, though, that Michael would start drinking because he had always expressed disdain for alcohol and drugs.

Over the next few years, Michael wrecked and totaled several cars and received two different OVIs, finally losing his driver's license for three years. Losing his license was an absolute blessing. He also spent a couple of weekends in jail. Amazingly after about three years, he gave up drinking as suddenly as he had started.

Sherry and I had moved Michael into his own apartment, more for our own sakes than for his. He still spent almost every evening and weekend with us. Michael didn't have active friendships anymore, and I think that he was lonely. He clung to me as his best friend, probably because he felt accepted and loved, even in the midst of his numerous problems.

One Saturday afternoon, Michael was in the upstairs of our home. I was in our living room when he yelled down to me. As I turned to see what he wanted, I saw him fall from the top of the stairway. He touched the stairs only once halfway down and slammed onto the floor at the bottom. He lay unconscious and then started to convulse, shaking violently. I called 911 because I didn't know what else to do. I didn't know if his prior brain injury might put him in greater danger from a fall than an average person.

As he lay there convulsing, I cried out, "Lord Jesus, please help my son." Immediately, the shaking and convulsing stopped.

The medics arrived and took him to the hospital. After Michael regained consciousness, he appeared to be all right.

CHAPTER 16

This was the beginning, though, of a new very serious problem. Michael began having grand mal seizures. Some people are able to sense when they are about to have a seizure, but Michael's seizures would occur without any warning. I'm thankful that he didn't have his driver's license anymore because he could easily have had a seizure while driving.

The seizures became progressively worse. We kept a close eye on Michael, contacting him throughout each day to make sure that he was all right. On more than one occasion, we found him after a seizure. He would be in his apartment, totally disoriented or unconscious, lying on the floor.

Sometimes he would remain unconscious for one or two days, finally waking in the hospital, disoriented, delusional, and many times belligerent. This confused condition could last for several days before he appeared to be normal again.

On four different occasions, he was so mentally impaired after a seizure that he had to be admitted to psychiatric hospitals for days or weeks. On one particular occasion, he had been recovering at OSU East Hospital for a couple of days after having seized. When he was released, I picked him up and took him back to his apartment. It was New Year's Eve 2010. Michael was going to spend the evening with us. Sherry and I picked him back up and took him to dinner. We all went back to our home and played several board games, finally ending our evening early because Michael was tired. I drove him back to his apartment and headed back home.

Michael called me the next morning at about six o'clock and told me that he felt like he was dying. Dying was a fear that he had developed because of the seizures. Michael spent much too much time bothering the local EMTs with calls.

I went over to his apartment and arrived just in time to see the medics leaving and chastising him again for calling them without a good reason. The medic in charge threatened to report Michael if he didn't stop calling 911 without a legitimate cause. It seemed that Michael was fine physically but not emotionally or mentally. I took Michael back home with me because he was still worried about how he was feeling.

Our three grandchildren were visiting and were at our house asleep, so I told Michael that he could lie on the couch in our living room to rest, and I would stay in the chair next to him to make sure that he was all right.

Sherry woke up shortly after eight o'çlock and came out of our bedroom. She suggested that Michael go and lie down in our bed so that when the grandchildren woke up, they wouldn't be a bother to him.

Sherry went into our bedroom about thirty minutes later to grab some clothes out of our closet when Michael objected. "Mom, don't go in the closet. Someone's in there waiting to kill you."

She came out of the bedroom and told me what he had said, so I went in. Michael told me, "Dad, someone's in the closet waiting to kill Mom." I knew that we were again in trouble.

We took Michael back to the same hospital that he left the day before. The hospital staff took him into the emergency room for observation for most of the day. Sherry and I went home but returned to the hospital later that afternoon.

The emergency room doctor met with us and told us that they couldn't find anything physically wrong with Michael. I asked him if they had checked his blood chemistry, and he said that they did, and everything appeared to be normal.

When we went into the emergency room to see him, he was scared and in tears. He told me, "Dad, I was wrong about my salvation. I'm in Hell."

"Michael, you're fine. You're not in Hell." We both assured him.

"Yes, I am. I must be in Hell because I can't leave…Dad." He sobbed. He was terrified! He believed that he was spiritually lost, and we couldn't convince him otherwise.

The emergency room doctor seemed oddly apathetic about our situation. He told Sherry and me, "We can't admit him because there isn't anything physically wrong with him."

Sherry and I didn't know what to do. We certainly couldn't take him back home with us in this mental state. The doctor seemed to show a little more compassion and told us that Michael needed to be sent to Netcare, an emergency mental health facility in downtown Columbus. They called for a medical transport to pick Michael up. When he was admitted to Netcare, we were not allowed to see him right away.

I was able to talk to him by phone the next morning. "Dad, can you get me out of here?" He begged.

"No, Michael," I told him. "You need to stay there so that they can find out what's going on with you."

"Dad, you have to get me out of here." He pleaded.

I tried to convince him that he had to stay there until the physicians at Netcare felt that it was safe to release him. In his mental condition, he envisioned me going with guns blazing to break him out by force.

I assured him that I wasn't going to do that, but I did promise that we would come and see him as soon as they allowed us to.

When we were able to visit Michael, I understood why he wanted to leave. Netcare consisted of a large room with a medical staff workstation in the center. The room was surrounded by small open-faced patient rooms. Each patient room contained a mattress on the floor, and that was about it. No box springs, bed frames, televisions, or chairs—nothing that could be used to assist a patient in harming themselves. Netcare existed purely for the purpose of emergency mental health evaluation. The psychiatrists could keep each patient for up to seventy-two hours and then determine what course of action was needed to treat each individual that was there.

When we finally saw Michael, he was still convinced that he was lost and in hell. I was becoming fearful that this delusion that he was experiencing might be permanent. They kept Michael at Netcare for two days and then transferred him to Twin Valley Hospital (a psychiatric hospital in West Columbus) for observation and treatment.

Twin Valley Hospital provided excellent care for Michael while he was there. Sherry and I discussed Michael's bulimia with one of the psychiatrists there, but he couldn't provide any solutions for Michael's eating disorder. Again they felt that Michael needed to be placed in inpatient care at a hospital that specialized in such conditions.

When Michael's blood chemistry improved from the lack of purging, so did his mental state. Michael finally understood that he wasn't in Hell. He was kept at Twin Valley for about ten days.

I did learn that if a person's blood sodium level drops too low, this type of delusional condition can occur. Michael seemed to finally come out of that event unharmed, but more problems were on the way.

Three additional times after having seizures, Michael was so mentally disoriented that he had to be placed in psychiatric care. Once he was again admitted to Twin Valley, and twice he was admitted to OSU's Harding Hospital (The Ohio State Universities psychiatric treatment facility). He received excellent care both at Twin Valley and Harding Hospital for the effects from the seizures, but no solution for treating Michael's bulimia was found.

The doctors believed that his purging was most likely the cause of the seizures. The hospital social workers did try to find help for his terrible addiction, but most support programs for eating disorders are understandably designed for women.

Michael also had the tendency to reject help because he felt that no one really understood his problem. He didn't believe that anyone *could* help him. I've been told that a person involved in an addiction like bulimia has to really be ready to give it up before they can, or until God intervenes to end it.

CHAPTER 17

It was now late fall, 2011. Seven years had passed since Michael had his motorcycle accident and ten years since he became anorexic/bulimic. He had experienced twenty or more grand mal seizures, and I'm sure that he had spent more than six months in hospitals.

Michael was living with Sherry and me again because he had been diagnosed as having acute seizure disorder. He was placed on permanent disability and needed to be closely monitored.

Michael had matured quite a lot and was much more pleasant to be with. His mind seemed to be functioning almost normally, but he had developed severe short-term memory problems. When we would go out to dinner, he, of course, would tag along. He would normally finish his dinner first and then tell us that his hands were sticky and that he needed to go to the restroom to wash. We knew that he really was going to the bathroom to purge his meal. When he was done, he would often need to call my cell phone to find out where we were sitting because he couldn't remember.

At about this time, Michael wanted to try cruising. He had saved some money and decided to go on a cruise to Mexico. He didn't have a passport but was able to cruise with just his birth certificate. I didn't know what might happen since he had short-term memory problems. He went alone because he now had no friends to go with him.

Michael went on his first cruise and loved it. He actually did all right getting to and from each port of call. He was safe traveling with just his birth certificate as long as he didn't get into trouble in a foreign country or miss re-boarding his ship before it left port. If that occurred, without having a passport, he would have been stuck in whatever foreign country he was in. Michael went on several cruises and made each one back home safely. I know that God watched over him, not only for his sake but for ours as well.

His bulimia wasn't as all-consuming as it was in his teen years, but his body was older and was not as forgiving. As with many people that have addictions, Michael seemed to feel that he could control his bulimia, but instead it *always* controlled him.

He and I would sometimes sit and talk about his problem. I cautioned him that he could easily have a stroke and end up in a nursing home for the rest of his life. He would just sit and nod somberly. I know that he was miserable because his life was so controlled by such a nasty and dangerous addiction, but he couldn't help it. He even said that he would now be willing to go to an inpatient clinic, but because he was an adult, the funding was no longer available. There was nothing Sherry or I could do.

I believe that, when we reached that point of absolute helplessness, it was the time that God stepped in and took complete control. It's almost as if He waited for us to get out of the way so that He could accomplish His will.

We also needed to come to a time of acceptance, trusting that God's decision in how to deal with our burden was what was best. It's very difficult to surrender our problems to the Lord and completely leave those problems at His feet and not pick them up again. The act of surrender is a day-by-day decision that we have to make, and that daily decision defines our faith.

CHAPTER 18

The day did come that the Lord Jesus took the final steps to save Michael's life.

I understand that shepherds of old who had a lamb that would constantly stray, would sometimes take the lamb and break one of its legs. The shepherd would mend the leg and then carry the lamb on his shoulders. He would hand-feed and lovingly care for the lamb until the leg was healed. From that time forward, the lamb would stay with the shepherd and never stray again. Though harsh, by breaking the lamb's leg, he would end up saving its life. By staying close to the shepherd, the lamb would be protected from wolves and other dangers.

I believe that Michael was a type of wandering lamb and Jesus was the Good Shepherd. God needed to stop Michael's bulimia, or it eventually would have killed him.

The remainder of this story reveals God's way of demonstrating His loving mercy for our son, for Sherry, and for me.

CHAPTER 19

Early one Monday morning in mid-July 2012, Michael didn't get out of bed. I knocked on his bedroom door but heard no response. I went into his room and immediately knew that he had suffered from another seizure. I called 911, and a squad came quickly.

As my reaction had always been, I questioned God, crying inside and not understanding why these problems continued to go on and on. Something, though, about this incident was different and more serious.

The medics hurried Michael to the squad where he was immediately put on a ventilator. Michael was moving when I opened his bedroom door, so I assumed that this was just another seizure, but it wasn't. They rushed Michael to the OSU Hospital emergency room. The medical team performed a CT scan of his brain to see if they could find out what had occurred.

At first, they thought that Michael might have had a stroke, but after doing blood work, that didn't appear to be what had happened. Whatever the cause, one thing was now clear: Michael had sustained a second brain injury. The first injury occurred in the front right lobe of the brain. This second injury occurred in the left side of his brain. This new injury was about to create a whole set of new and different challenges for Sherry and me.

A day or so passed before Michael regained consciousness. When he finally did, one of the first things we noticed was that he wasn't able to talk. He would stare straight ahead but could not respond to stimulation. The doctors believed that Michael's second brain injury was caused by anoxia—lack of oxygen to the brain. No one knew what could have caused the anoxia, but the doctors didn't know what else would have led to this second brain injury.

By this time, Sherry and I had almost become numb to bad news about our son. We told the doctors that this wasn't Michael's first brain injury and that we believed God would pull him through this. We were confident that after time he would be all right.

Then his doctor gave us the tragic news. An anoxic brain injury is very different from the impact brain injury that Michael received during his motorcycle accident. Anoxic brain injuries don't normally heal very well, *if at all.*

Sherry and I were stunned. We didn't know what to think. Living with Michael's bulimia was difficult enough. We didn't know what we would do now that Michael might be permanently disabled. Along with his lack of ability to talk, he was showing no signs of movement on his right side, which might now be paralyzed.

We visited Michael every day hoping to see some improvement in his condition. Several days passed before we saw any changes. The nurses who were working with Michael did finally notice that with stimulation, Michael would wiggle his toes. It wasn't long before he started displaying movement in his legs.

Michael began to slowly respond to other stimulation. He would look at us when we talked to him. Soon he could stand and then walk slowly with assistance.

The nurses told Michael that there was a bowl of candy in a doctor's office down the hall. Apparently, he understood what they were saying because that was all of the motivation he needed to work on his walking. With a nurse on either side helping him, he moved as quickly as he could to get some of that candy. He also began to muster a word or two, but his speech was virtually nonexistent.

After several weeks of limited improvement, the hospital decided that it was time for Michael to leave. He needed to be placed in full-time nursing care. We decided to send him to a nursing home close to where we lived. This nursing home was, like most nursing homes, filled primarily with the elderly.

By this time, Michael had become pretty mobile. He could walk without assistance. He was still very confused and was unable to communicate. The doctors determined that Michael was suffering from a form of dementia.

I went to visit Michael at around nine o'clock one evening. When I walked into his room, he was having what appeared to be a seizure. His arm was elevated, and he was trembling. I rushed out to get a nurse from the nurse's desk.

She walked in and watched Michael for a few moments and then walked off, saying that she didn't think that he was seizing. I couldn't believe it. Again I asked God to help Michael. When I spoke the name of Jesus, the trembling stopped, and he appeared to fall asleep. After that, I was very concerned about the lack of care that he might be receiving at that nursing home.

There was also the danger that if he could get out of the building, he might wander off and become lost. They put a sensor on his ankle that would set off an alarm and lock any exterior door he was trying to go through if he made it past the nurse's desk.

It was just a few days before the nursing home had enough of our son. Michael's whole goal was to escape this prison that he was in, and he tried again and again to do so. I have no idea where he thought he was going to go if he got out of the building, but he was determined to get away.

CHAPTER 20

A social worker at the nursing home decided to try to have Michael admitted to Dodd Hall at OSU Hospital again, hoping that their expertise in rehabilitation might help. Dodd accepted him on a very temporary basis. We were told that the current policy at Dodd was to keep patients no longer than fourteen days. Again they took very good care of Michael, assigning a tech to be with him almost all of the time.

We hoped that the physicians at Dodd would be able to provide some sort of treatment that might help Michael return to a more normal state of mind. They found that Michael wouldn't or couldn't participate in any type of rehabilitation. Because of this, Dodd couldn't allow him to stay. Social workers at OSU located another nursing home that they believed could care for Michael. Instead of being full of just the elderly, this facility had behavioral units for people of multiple ages and with various problems.

Sherry and I were sure to visit Michael there every day. This particular nursing home was secured, so there was no chance of him running off. The care there was adequate at best. It was not staffed very well, and the environment was depressing. I've come to see how lonely nursing homes are for many people, those who have no one to care about what happens to them or to visit when they are lonely. It seems that many people are just left in nursing homes to die.

We had no other choice but to leave Michael there, but we made sure that he knew that he was loved. When we would go to visit him each day, we would sign in the visitor's book at the building's entrance. Sometimes no other signatures would be in the book between our visits, meaning that no one else had received any visitors.

Sherry and I finally took a break, going on a short but very needed vacation, trusting that Michael would be all right. Everything seemed to go well while we were gone. When we returned, we went to see Michael. As I was standing and talking to him, his demeanor suddenly changed. He stared intently into my eyes, took his left hand, and palm-punched me in the chest. Michael is right-handed, and though the seizure had caused his right arm and hand to be partially paralyzed, his left hand was fully functional and moved quickly.

Michael again stared blankly into my eyes and hit me hard. He backed off and got a strange smile on his face and said the word *kidding*, and then he hugged me. A few minutes later, he hit me again and then tried to hit Sherry.

From that point on, we didn't know what to expect. Each day when we would visit him, he would at first seem all right, but then he would become aggressive and try to hit with that one good hand.

Michael started hitting staff members at the nursing home in the same fashion. It wasn't long before this facility called us to say that Michael could not stay there either. Sherry also received a call from a doctor associated with the Ohio State Universities Medical Department, a family practitioner who had been treating Michael before this second devastating anoxia injury. She had checked on him through Ohio States medical records and found out about his latest brain injury.

She knew about the nursing facility that Michael was in and wanted us to immediately remove him from there. She told us to take him back to the emergency room at OSU Hospital and she would have him admitted into Harding Hospital. Harding is the psychiatric hospital at Ohio State where Michael had been admitted twice before for short stays. She wanted him to remain at Harding until an appropriate permanent home could be found for him.

The day that she contacted us was the same day that we received the call from the nursing facility Michael was staying in, telling us that he had to be relocated. We were thrilled that this doctor was directing us to take him back to Harding for treatment because we wanted him out of the nursing home, and we felt that Harding was an excellent place for Michael to go.

We went that afternoon and permanently removed him from the nursing home and took him back to OSU's emergency room and waited. We explained to the ER staff what we were instructed by the doctor to do. Michael was a handful to deal with while we waited for them to admit him back into Harding. He was antsy most of the time. It took about six hours of waiting for someone from Harding to come and tell us that they weren't sure whether they could admit Michael again or not.

Now we were in a quandary. We had just permanently removed Michael from the nursing facility that he had been in. If Harding wouldn't admit him, we had no place else to take him. We could not take care of him ourselves. The situation would have been almost laughable if it were not so serious.

After spending nearly eight hours in the emergency room dealing with our son, we were exhausted! He was *very* active and restless.

At about two o'clock in the morning, Sherry and I decided to leave Michael in the hands of the emergency room staff and went home to rest. The hospital called at around four thirty that morning and told us that Michael *was* being admitted to Harding again. What a relief and an answer to prayer.

We continued to see God's merciful hand working in Michael's life. An average stay at Harding Hospital is normally limited to two weeks. Michael was allowed to stay for ten weeks because no place else was found that could or would take care of him. A problem can arise if a loved one is rejected by several nursing homes for one reason or another, a reputation can develop in the nursing home community against that person and then it can be very hard to find a home that will accept them.

Michael showed very limited progress while he was at Harding Hospital. His vocabulary improved a little, and the functioning of his right side was slightly better. He still had a minor problem with his right leg. His right hand and arm were still very dysfunctional. Michael also had almost no vocabulary or short-term memory, and he couldn't read or write. By this time, Sherry and I had accepted the fact that this was going to be his permanent condition.

CHAPTER 21

The day finally arrived when Michael had to leave Harding Hospital. He was now showing no appreciable signs of improvement, and the space at Harding was needed for other patients. A social worker at OSU located a facility in Cleveland that would accept Michael as a resident. Harding arranged for his transportation, and off he went.

We went to see him in Cleveland that same evening. This facility was near the Cleveland Clinic, a two-hour drive from our Westerville, Ohio, home. What we found was very disappointing. The facility appeared to be housing primarily for the poor, the homeless, and ex-cons, not for people with traumatic brain injuries. It also seemed to be understaffed.

There was a large common room where there were vending machines for the residents to buy snacks, but no one seemed to have any money. When we went in, we were barraged by people asking for change. We couldn't leave food for Michael in his room because he wouldn't remember where we put it. If we left snacks or cans of soda out where it could be seen by him, it would be taken by others.

We noticed that Michael had gotten sick on his shared bathroom floor. He still had a problem with reflux, which means that he had trained his body so efficiently to purge, that food would involuntarily come back up into his mouth where he would chew it up again and swallow it. Sometimes though he would drop or spit it out of his mouth. That was most likely the cause rather than bulimic purging. Sherry did her best to clean it up with paper towels. When we returned two days later, it still hadn't been mopped up properly.

We were heartsick. When you love your children, you want them to be safe, happy, and well taken care of, especially when they are helpless. This facility wasn't the place for that. Up until coming to this home, Michael had almost constantly received one-on-one care, meaning that someone had personally been with him almost all of the time. We were now very concerned because he was helpless and would be *unsupervised* most of the time. Michael could not even find his own room. We prayed with him and left him in Jesus's hands.

We were on the verge of tears as we prepared to go home. I asked a male nurse at the nursing station if he would make sure Michael was taken care of. I'm sure he could see the worry in my eyes as they were beginning to tear up. He said to me, "Yes, in Jesus's name, I will." I was so thankful for that assurance.

I am reminded about how God spoke to my heart when Michael was on the train in Chicago, telling me, "You're helpless. You're going to have to depend on me." Those words from God have become the crutch that I lean on every day. We *are* helpless in our weakness, but I know that God's strength is made perfect in our weakness.

CHAPTER 22

Sherry and I knew that we couldn't allow Michael to stay in Cleveland in that environment. We began searching for someplace new for him to go to on our own. A business acquaintance of ours suggested that we try contacting Majora Lane nursing home in Millersburg, Ohio. The small city of Millersburg borders Ohio's Amish community of Berlin, a beautiful and very peaceful area.

Sherry called the facility and went to take a look the next morning. It seemed to be clean and homey, and the staff was courteous and professional. They sent a representative to interview Michael and felt like it was a workable situation to accept him as a resident. We transferred Michael as quickly as possible, feeling good about this new environment.

Living at Majora Lane lasted for about four weeks until the staff became concerned about Michael's activity level around the elderly patients. Again it was decided that it wasn't going to work out. They did have one recommendation. Seville Meadows, a nursing facility in Seville, Ohio, had an opening in their behavioral care unit that sounded like it could work. It would be our fifth attempt to place Michael in a full-care nursing facility. Seville Meadows is located in a small, northern Ohio farming community falling between Columbus and Cleveland. Like the nursing home in Millersburg, Seville Meadows was well staffed. Someone went and interviewed Michael and accepted him as a resident.

CHAPTER 23

I thank God for providing this new home for our son. It turned out to be a good fit for Michael. The behavioral unit was perfect. It was very secure. There was a courtyard where Michael could safely go to and enjoy the outdoors. It was full of people who, like Michael, have experienced some type of severe brain trauma. The staff is professional and kind. It appeared that Michael was finally home.

Michael has now been at Seville Meadows for almost four years. We have come to know and treasure the staff who watches over our son. They understand his issues and work with him patiently. We are able to call him daily and visit him weekly.

We always try to take Michael out for lunch when we go to visit. Sometimes he'll walk up to the restaurant counter to order his own food and then realize that he doesn't have the words in his vocabulary to say what he wants. He'll motion for us to order for him, or he'll just say, "You decide," and he'll let us select his meal.

Seville meadows is just about a hundred miles north of our home. When we drive up to see Michael, we always take goodies for him and the other patients in his unit, many of whom we have come to know and enjoy seeing. Some of them are very lonely people who have little to look forward to other than when someone takes a moment to say hello and gives them a small treat to break the monotony of the day.

When we visit Michael and he sees us come into his unit, he gets a big grin on his face, especially when he sees his mother that he loves so much. He always has hugs and kisses for each of us. His speech is very limited, but he always tells us that he loves us. Sometimes he'll say he's coming home.

CHAPTER 24

This is not the end to the story of Michael's life since his dieting began. He does seem happy, free from the burden of his bulimia. Michael, though, will never again have the opportunity to do the things that most men his age are able to do.

The purging had damaged his teeth so severely that he had to have half of them surgically removed. The remainder are shrunken due to erosion from his stomach acids. His purging had also damaged his esophagus almost to the point of rupturing. Michael will never date, drive again, or be independent. He has paid a horrible price for his addiction.

Sherry and I do see improvements in Michael's brain function each time that we visit him. We had been told that a brain injury will normally improve for the first two years after it occurs, but after that, the improvements generally slow or stop, but we are still seeing healing after four years. I do praise the Lord for that.

As I consider my past faults and shortcomings as Michael's father, there are so many things that I might have done differently. They say that hindsight is twenty-twenty, and that is very true. I have to trust, though, that God has guided and directed the events in our lives to keep us on our knees, causing us to seek Him without ceasing because of our helplessness. Sherry and I have witnessed so many direct answers to prayer while dealing with Michael's problems. Through the hurt that we have experienced, we have also seen God grow our faith and trust in Him.

I do desire to see Michael become free from the bondage of his injury if that is part of the Lord's plan for his life, but I would not want Michael to be outside of the will and wisdom of the Lord. We still have challenges with our son and worries to deal with every day. He is an ever-present concern in our lives, but we love him. He is worth everything we go through. I'm so thankful that God saved his life. By human standards, Michael should have died, and maybe the part of his brain, the part that drove and empowered his illness, did die. But at least for now, he is alive, and for now, hopefully forever, the bulimia is gone. During the past fifteen years, we have gone through many dark days. On numerous occasions, I felt very alone and forgotten by God. He was still with me and my family, though, watching over us and caring for us. God knew the end of our situation with Michael before the day that his illness ever began.

Day by day, we still have our son. Day by day, the Lord Jesus carries Michael gently on His shoulders as a good shepherd carries a broken lamb. Each day Jesus leads and watches over *all* of His lambs, all of those that put their faith and trust in Him. When we do wander, He follows us and takes us back to Himself, making sure that we never stray too far again.

CONCLUSION

My final question: are you in the flock of Jesus? Have you asked Jesus to be your Lord and Savior?

Almost every person on earth has heard of Jesus. Some love Him. Some hate Him. Some admire Him, but from a distance. Many go to church each week to worship Him, but not everyone belongs to Him.

The apostle John tells us, "There was a man of the Pharisees named Nicodemus, a ruler of the Jews; the same came to Jesus by night and said unto him, "Rabbi, we know that thou art a teacher come from God: for no man can do these miracles that thou doest, except God be with him. Jesus answered and said unto him, "Verily, verily, I say unto thee, except a man be born again, he cannot see the kingdom of God."

Jesus understood what Nicodemus was wanting to know before he asked. It was the same question that we all have. What happens after death? Jesus wanted Nicodemus to recognize that something needs to occur in a person's life to gain forgiveness for sin and to receive everlasting life. A person must experience a new birth, a spiritual birth to belong to Christ.

This new life begins when we become part of Jesus's flock and He becomes our shepherd. Only then are we really one of Gods children. When Jesus was crucified, he was hung on a cross between two criminals, both had committed crimes worthy of death. God wanted us to understand that both of these men were essentially the same. They had lived Godless lives and were now facing certain death and eternal judgment.

As the day of crucifixion drew on, that solemn day of atonement when Jesus offered Himself as the sacrificial Lamb of God, one of the two criminals experienced a change of heart. He saw the events that were occurring around him. He witnessed the forgiving Spirit that Jesus was showing to those who were crucifying Him. This desperate man came to believe that Jesus was the king of Israel, that He was the Son of the Living God. While the other condemned man railed on Jesus, crying out, "If thou be Christ, save thyself and us," the penitent man rebuked him, saying, "Dost not thou fear God, seeing that thou art in the same condemnation? And we indeed justly, for we receive the due reward of our deeds, but this man hath done nothing amiss. And he said unto Jesus, Lord, remember me when thou comest into thy kingdom. And Jesus said unto him, Verily I say unto thee, Today shalt thou be with me in paradise."

Two men were crucified with Jesus that day. Two men with wasted lives. There was no longer time to make amends or to live righteously, only enough time to utter a simple prayer. Possibly a hopeless request for Jesus to accept, to forgive, and to remember this repentant man when Jesus entered into His kingdom. The man had nothing to offer God but his sins, a wasted empty life, and a prayer of faith, but that was all that God required of him.

Jesus accepted this hopeless man unconditionally because he accepted and trusted Jesus unconditionally. When he cried out to the Lord, he was accepted. Jesus forgave him of his sins and gave him the gift of eternal life. Two men died with Jesus that day. One accepted God's gift of forgiveness, and one did not. One went to be with Jesus in His kingdom that day, and one was forever lost.

Jesus wants you to belong to Him. He loves you so much that he was willingly arrested, cruelly mocked, spit upon, brutally beaten beyond recognition, and then killed by crucifixion. He suffered all of this to make Himself a sacrifice for your sin unto God. Jesus took the punishment that *we* deserved for *our* sins so that we wouldn't have to. On the third day, Jesus rose again from the dead to prove that our redemption to God was complete.

If you are not a lamb in Christ's fold, He wants you to be. He's waiting for you with open arms to take you to himself, if you will just turn your life over to Him. Ask Him in prayer to forgive you of your sins and to be your Lord and Savior. You'll receive the gift of eternal life, just like the penitent man that died with Jesus. The Holy Spirit will come and live inside you. It's Christ's promise that He will accept you, and you will belong to Him forever. Don't delay in accepting God's gift of salvation. Call upon the name of Jesus right now. Remember, 2 Corinthians 6:2 says, "Behold, *now* is the accepted time; behold, *now* is the day of salvation."

If you have made a decision to accept Jesus as your Lord and Savior, prayerfully seek out and attend a Bible-believing church that will help you grow in your faith and knowledge of God.

"For the wages of sin is death, but the gift of God is eternal life through Jesus Christ our Lord" (Romans 6:23).

"For whosoever shall call upon the name of the Lord shall be saved" (Romans 10:13).

ABOUT THE AUTHOR

J on Hunter is a self-employed carpet cleaner in central Ohio. Jon works with his oldest son, Gabriel, and Sherry, his loving wife of forty-two years. His youngest son, Michael, lives in a nursing home in Seville, Ohio. Jon became a born-again Christian when he was twenty years old. He believes that other than his salvation, his family is his greatest gift from God.